The Quest for Reality

The Quest for Reality

Subjectivism and the

Metaphysics

of Colour

BARRY STROUD

New York   Oxford

Oxford University Press

2000

Oxford University Press

Oxford   New York
Athens   Auckland   Bangkok   Bogotá   Buenos Aires   Calcutta
Cape Town   Chennai   Dar es Salaam   Delhi   Florence   Hong Kong   Istanbul
Karachi   Kuala Lumpur   Madrid   Melbourne   Mexico City   Mumbai
Nairobi   Paris   São Paulo   Singapore   Taipei   Tokyo   Toronto   Warsaw

and associated companies in
Berlin   Ibadan

Copyright © 2000 by Barry Stroud

Published by Oxford University Press, Inc.
198 Madison Avenue, New York, New York 10016

Oxford is a registered trademark of Oxford University Press

Library of Congress Cataloging-in-Publication Data

Stroud, Barry.
The quest for reality : subjectivism and the metaphysics of colour
/ Barry Stroud.
p.   cm.
Based on the author's 1987 John Locke lectures
at Oxford University.
Includes bibliographical references and index.
ISBN 0-19-513388-9
1. Color (Philosophy)   I. Title.
B105.C455S77   2000
111—dc21   99-20505

1 3 5 7 9 8 6 4 2

Printed in the United States of America
on acid-free paper

For Julia, because . . .

This is how philosophers should salute each other:
"Take your time!"

—L. Wittgenstein

Preface

This book deals with a huge metaphysical enterprise. No one could treat it exhaustively in a single book—or lifetime—and I do not try to. I concentrate on drawing attention to what I think are some of its distinctive features and exploring one or two of them far enough to draw some tentative morals. I do not expect agreement from many philosophers, but I do hope even those with little sympathy towards what they find here are encouraged to look again at the task of reaching intelligible and reliable metaphysical conclusions.

I write out of the conviction that philosophy is extremely difficult. That would perhaps go without saying, did not so much recent philosophizing seem to me to proceed otherwise. I find it is especially true of treatments of some of the topics I try to investigate here.

One source of the difficulty is that responses to philosophical questions tend to start too late. J. L. Austin is reported to have observed that in works of philosophy it is usually all over by the bottom of page one. I think that is right and can be confirmed by more or less random reading. What really matters is off the page and settled in the mind before the author's announced task has even begun. Here I try to go into the sources of some of the questions I take up, but without supposing that I get far enough to avoid the inveterate tendency in my own case.

Another conviction out of which I write is that philosophy is one subject and that progress in one place depends on the resolution of issues that lie elsewhere. One is led eventually into almost all other areas and questions. This is certainly true of the work of the great philosophers of the past. Against that high standard, the current professional fixation on distinct "fields" or areas of academic "specialization" and "competence" looks like no more than a bad joke. It would be more amusing if it were not having such disastrous effects on philosophy and on intellectual life generally.

These convictions express part of my sense of the special character of philosophical problems and doctrines and of the difficulty of recognizing that character and describing or explaining it in the right way. Many philosophers do not pay much attention to this. Either they think they understand it well enough already, or they recognize no significant difference between philosophy and other efforts to get to know something. In any case, they are too busy trying to answer their philosophical questions to spend much time on where they come from.

Investigating the philosophical quest for reality as I do here is one way of pursuing the question of what philosophy is meant to do, at least if it takes the form of philosophical doctrine or theory. The very notion of a philosophical theory or thesis or doctrine is something I wish to understand better than I do. We cannot simply define the idea of the philosophical at the outset and then look for views or doctrines that fulfill that definition. No form of words alone can serve to identify a remark or a thought as philosophical. We must understand the task or question those words or thoughts are a response to and how they are meant to be taken for the particular philosophical purpose at hand.

I do think there is something that philosophy aspires to which needs to be identified and described and understood. Or, rather, I think there is something human beings aspire to which finds its expression in philosophy. We seek a certain kind of understanding of ourselves and of reality that will make intelligible to us in general terms the relation in which we stand to that reality—or perhaps the relation in which we really stand to it. But to describe the goal in this shorthand way is to make essential use of the very idea of reality that I want to explore. Can we get any independent understanding of it? Our grasp of the idea probably cannot be separated from our ability to understand and carry out the kind of project I am interested in. The quest for reality and the goal of philosophy are too closely connected for one of them to be much help in explaining the other.

Obviously, I cannot take up the quest wherever it has made its appearance. After identifying some of its general features, I concentrate on one particular area and hope that it will serve as an instructive example. What I have to say, if found plausible, might eventually encourage the suspicion that, at least within the area I consider, there might never be a philosophical theory or doctrine that could fully satisfy our philosophical desire to understand. That is not something I argue for directly. For one thing, to try to establish it, I would have to say something pretty definite about what the suspicion amounts to. I would have to explain what a philosophical theory or doctrine is supposed to be. And to explain why such a thing could never satisfy us, I would have to say what it would be for a philosophical theory to satisfy us. That would mean identifying and describing what we seek or aspire to in philosophy. And that is just my problem. That is what this book is about.

There is a further reason for not trying to prove that no satisfactory philosophical theory is possible in this area. If it could be established at all, it would presumably be something of a philosophical theory or doctrine in its own right. It would therefore imply that if it is true it could never satisfy us; if it did satisfy us, it could not be true. I do not try to prove or even to argue for such a bold antitheoretical thesis, even in the restricted area I have chosen. I simply try to draw attention to the very special character of a philosophical theory or doctrine of the kind we seek and to identify some of the ideas we rely on in taking it for granted that such a thing is possible.

I do hope that in my efforts in that direction I say only what is true, even if it is too much to expect it to be found satisfying. For many readers, I know, my efforts will seem too negative, too noncommittal—in a word, too untheoretical. I am familiar with that reaction, and I try not to be defensive in the face of it. I think much more careful work is needed right back at the beginnings of the philosophical questions that grip us—at the earliest fundamentals, as it were—before we can be sure that we know what we are doing. Only then can we try to do it in the right way. My worry is rather that I do not get deeply enough even into those fundamentals. I certainly do not get as far as offering answers of my own to philosophical questions about reality. But I hope my reasons for finding puzzling the very idea of a philosophical theory of reality prove to be philosophically rewarding.

My interest in the question does not come from a wish to put an end to the search for intellectually satisfying philosophical theories, or even to discourage it or limit its range. Quite the contrary. I believe that the urge to achieve the kind of view of ourselves and the world that is embodied in the philosophical quest for reality arises from something deeper in human nature than any abstract argument against it is ever likely to reach. It is present in all our best efforts to understand ourselves and will probably always be with us. I think it is idle to try either to discourage or to encourage philosophical theorizing about the human condition. The point is to understand what it is and what it aspires to.

The only seed of doubt I would be pleased to sow is the suspicion that perhaps the goal is not fully reachable, that the kind of understanding of ourselves and the world that is embodied in that quest is not really available to us. Not because of ignorance, difficulty, or limited capacities—all of which are familiar enough—but because of the very nature of the task. That is at least a possibility I would like to keep alive. Finding something like that to be so, or even having reason to suspect that it might be, could in itself amount to an illuminating form of self-understanding—perhaps the best we can hope for.

Any movement either towards or away from that conclusion can be based only on a detailed scrutiny of specific applications of what I am calling the quest for reality. There is no settling the matter *a priori* and once and for all. Sixty years ago, metaphysical theorizing was declared meaningless on the sweeping grounds that its results were neither true by virtue of meaning alone nor confirmable or disconfirmable in experience. But metaphysical theorizing of the proscribed kind was involved in reaching that very conclusion. It proved to be essential to philosophy then just as it is today, in what in some quarters are still proudly thought to be enlightened scientific times.

Nowadays one is more likely to find philosophical questions dismissed out of hand on the even more sweeping grounds that we are led to ask them only because we have come to think in certain ways—certain "contingent" ways of thinking, which, if things had been different, we might never have come to adopt at all. The implication is that if we simply abandon those old ways of thinking, the problems, or their urgency, will vanish. But that form of criticism as it stands is absurd. What it says about philosophical problems is true of all intellectual problems. Without some particular ways of thinking, we could never try to understand anything. It is a "contingent" fact, which could have been otherwise, that we now have such a thing as a quantum theory of matter, for example, or the theory of natural selection or number theory. But the "contingency" of those ways of thinking does not mean that any problems that arise within them are unreal or not worth a serious person's attention, or that if we cannot solve the problems we can simply abandon the ways of thinking that give rise to them. If philosophy is to be dismissed for the "contingency" of its problems or its ways of thinking, it must be shown how and why those ways of thinking and the problems they generate are somehow confused or idle or unintelligible or otherwise illegitimate. And the only way to show that in a convincing and illuminating way is to examine particular philosophical issues carefully, to identify and understand their special character, and to trace them convincingly to their sources.